Made in the USA
Monee, IL
27 August 2021

76654991R00057